The Attributes of Jesus 30 Day Devotional

Nichol Collins

Copyright © 2024

This book or parts thereof may not be reproduced in any form, stored in a retrieval system, or transmitted in any form by any means; electronic, mechanical, photocopying, recording, or otherwise, is not permitted without prior written permission of the author.

All Rights Reserved 2024
ISBN 978-1-965553-05-3
Globe Shakers Publishing Co.
Globeshakers.com

Other Books

Amazon links on Website
https://globeshakers.com/pages/authors-corner
-Behind Enemy Lines (autobiography)
-I See Through Muddy Water (Signs of Down Low Men)
-Power: The Benefits of Speaking in Tongues
-Church Politics Vol. 1-4 The Mafia, Greed, Perverseness, Compromise
-Under Construction: Men's LGBT Deliverance Manual
-No Residue: Women's LGBT Deliverance Manual
-Reaching the LGBT: Effective Evangelism
-Walking in Power 30 Day Devotional
-Attributes of Jesus 30 Day Devotional
-The Seek 30 Day Devotional

-Numerous Children's Books combating the LGBT agenda, abuse, and self esteem

Yevette Fisher's Books (My Mom)
-Devil Let My Baby Go
-Momma's Last Breath
-What About Conrad
-Holy Toledo
-No One is Exempt
-Walk by Faith Prayer Journal
-In Between Trains

Table of Contents

Day 1: Jesus, the Savior	1
Day 2: Jesus, the Healer	4
Day 3: Jesus, Good Shepherd	7
Day 4: Jesus, the Bread of Life	9
Day 5: Jesus, Light of the World	12
Day 6: Jesus, Prince of Peace	14
Day 7: Jesus, the Way	17
Day 8: Jesus, the Truth	20
Day 9: Jesus, the Life	23
Day 10: Jesus, the Lamb of God	25
Day 11: Jesus, the Vine	27
Day 12: Jesus, the Word	30
Day 13: Jesus, Emmanuel	32
Day 14: Jesus, the Redeemer	34
Day 15: Jesus, the King of Kings	36
Day 16: Jesus, the Servant	38
Day 17: Jesus, Miracle Worker	40
Day 18: Jesus, the Advocate	42
Day 19: Jesus, the Friend	44
Day 20: Jesus, the Alpha Omega	46
Day 21: Jesus, the Judge	48
Day 22: Jesus, the Teacher	50
Day 23: Jesus, the Lion of Judah	52
Day 24: Jesus, the Intercessor	54
Day 25: Jesus, the Rock	56
Day 26: Jesus, the Bridegroom	58
Day 27: Jesus, the High Priest	61
Day 28: Jesus, Fullness of God	63
Day 29: Jesus, One w/the Father	66
Day 30: Jesus, My Deliverer	69

Nichol Collins

Day 1: Jesus, the Savior

"She will give birth to a son, and you are to give him the name Jesus, because he will save his people from their sins." – Matthew 1:21

From the moment sin entered the world through Adam and Eve, God's plan of salvation was set into motion. Jesus, whose very name means "The Lord Saves," is the manifestation of God Himself in flesh, fulfilling His promise to redeem humanity. As the one true God revealed in Christ, He came to save and reconcile us to Himself. Jesus didn't come to condemn us for our sins but to save us from the wrath to come, offering a path to forgiveness, reconciliation, and eternal life.

His mission was clear: to rescue us from the penalty of sin, which is death, and to break the power of sin that holds us captive. This required

The Attributes of Jesus

Him to leave His heavenly throne, take on human flesh, and endure unimaginable suffering on the cross. It wasn't just nails that held Him there—it was His love for you and me. He willingly endured the punishment we deserved, becoming the ultimate sacrifice so we could be restored to a right relationship with God.

Take a moment today to reflect on the depth of Jesus' love for you. Imagine the weight of the cross He carried, not just physically but spiritually, as He took upon Himself the sins of the entire world. Picture His outstretched arms on Calvary, signifying that His salvation is available to all who will receive it.

Through Jesus, we are not only saved from sin, but we are also saved for a purpose—to live a life that glorifies Him and shares His love with others. Let this truth inspire you to walk in the freedom, joy, and gratitude that comes from knowing you are saved by grace.

Are there areas in your life where you struggle to fully embrace Jesus' forgiveness?

Nichol Collins

The Lord says, "He loves you unconditionally, and the sooner you align with His love, the freer you will become from the opinions of others. Stay humble but confident in Calvary, knowing your sins are under the blood."

The Attributes of Jesus

Day 2: Jesus, the Healer

"But he was wounded for our transgressions, he was bruised for our iniquities: the chastisement of our peace was upon him; and with his stripes we are healed." – Isaiah 53:5

Jesus, as the Healer, brings restoration and wholeness to every area of our lives. Isaiah 53:5 reveals the depth of His sacrifice, emphasizing that His suffering on the cross was not only for our sins but also for our healing. Through His wounds, we are made whole—physically, emotionally, psychologically, and spiritually.

Physical healing is a visible demonstration of Jesus' power. Throughout His ministry, He healed the sick, opened blind eyes, and even raised the dead. These miracles were not merely acts of compassion but signs of His authority as God in the flesh among us. Today, we can trust

Him as the same Healer, knowing that His power has not diminished.

Emotionally, Jesus heals the wounds of the heart. Life can leave us broken, carrying burdens of grief, shame, and rejection. But Jesus offers peace to the troubled soul, binding up the brokenhearted and bringing comfort to those who mourn (Isaiah 61:1-3).

Psychological healing through Jesus addresses the battlefield of the mind, bringing peace to areas of anxiety, trauma, and confusion. By surrendering our burdens to Him, we experience renewed clarity, hope, and a transformed mindset rooted in His truth.

Spiritually, the ultimate healing comes through the forgiveness of sin. Our greatest need is to be reconciled to God, and through His death and resurrection, Jesus provided the way. He heals the spiritual separation caused by sin, restoring us to right standing with God and granting us eternal life. As we are identified with Him, we obey Acts 2:38—turning from sin, burying it in baptism for remission, and being renewed through the infilling of the Holy Spirit.

The Attributes of Jesus

Jesus is the Healer who makes all things new. His sacrifice ensures that restoration is available to all who come to Him in faith. Take a moment today to pray in the Spirit, allowing the Great Physician to minister to those areas. The Lord says, "Trust Him to bring restoration and wholeness into your life. I did not bring you to this point to abandon you."

Nichol Collins

Day 3: Jesus, the Good Shepherd

"I am the good shepherd. The good shepherd lays down his life for the sheep." – John 10:11

In the ancient world, shepherds had an intimate connection with their sheep. They knew each one by name, guided them to safe pastures, protected them from predators, and cared for them when they were injured or lost. Jesus describes Himself as the Good Shepherd who loves, leads, and sacrifices for His sheep—us.

As our Good Shepherd, Jesus provides for our every need. He leads us to spiritual nourishment, refreshes our weary souls, and offers protection from the enemy. He doesn't abandon us in times of trouble. Instead, He walks alongside us, even in the darkest valleys, reminding us that we are never alone. His guidance is perfect, and His care is unending.

The Attributes of Jesus

The most powerful expression of His love as the Good Shepherd is His willingness to lay down His life for us. Take comfort in knowing that Jesus is actively caring for you. He knows your struggles, fears, and desires. He calls you by name and as sheep, our role is to listen to His voice, follow His lead, and rest in the safety of His arms.

The Lord says, "Son, be of good cheer. My daughter, be not afraid of what lies ahead. I have you in the palm of My hand. I, the Lord, am leading you into green pastures, and your fruit shall not wither but remain. If you trust My plan, it will be evident that I heard you the first time. Rest in My bosom. I got you."

Nichol Collins

Day 4: Jesus, the Bread of Life

"Then Jesus declared, 'I am the bread of life. Whoever comes to me will never go hungry, and whoever believes in me will never be thirsty.'"
– John 6:35

In our physical lives, bread is often considered a fundamental food, something essential for nourishment and strength. Likewise, Jesus declares Himself as the "Bread of Life," revealing His role as the essential sustenance for our spiritual well-being. Just as bread satisfies physical hunger, Jesus satisfies the deepest hunger of our souls.

The world offers many distractions—success, relationships, or possessions—but none can truly satisfy our hearts. When we turn to Jesus and trust in His Word, He fills us with peace and purpose. His presence meets our deepest needs and nourishes us like nothing else.

The Attributes of Jesus

In John 6, Jesus was speaking to a crowd that had experienced the miraculous feeding of the five thousand. While they sought Him for more physical bread, Jesus redirected their focus to the eternal: *"Do not work for food that spoils, but for food that endures to eternal life"* (John 6:27). He was teaching them that He alone is the source of eternal life, and those who partake of Him will never hunger again.

To come to Jesus means to trust Him completely as our source of life. To believe in Him means to live in relationship with Him, feeding on His Word daily and allowing Him to transform us from the inside out. His invitation is open to all: "Whoever comes to me will never go hungry."

Are you spiritually hungry today? Are you longing for peace, fulfillment, or hope? Jesus offers Himself as the Bread of Life. In Him, you will find all that your soul longs for.

The Lord says, "Eat of His word for the nourishment you need. You feel weary because My word is not hidden within the inner corridors of your heart. Slow down a bit and prioritize dining on the Finest of Wheat—My word is going to fill the voids and be the spiritual multivitamin you are lacking as a boost to your endeavors. I am orchestrating this plan. Watch Me provide."

The Attributes of Jesus

Day 5: Jesus, the Light of the World

"When Jesus spoke again to the people, he said, 'I am the light of the world. Whoever follows me will never walk in darkness, but will have the light of life.'" – John 8:12

Light has the power to transform everything it touches. It clears the way, brings peace, and exposes the truth, dispelling the darkness and revealing what was once hidden. In John 8:12, Jesus declares Himself as the Light of the World, offering guidance to all who walk in the darkness of sin, confusion, or fear.

Jesus shines His light into the darkest corners of our lives, revealing the lies we've believed and the chains that bind us. His light uncovers the truth about God's love, our identity in Him, and the hope we have for eternal life. Without His light, we stumble, unsure of where we are going.

Nichol Collins

But with Him, we have a clear path to follow—a path that leads to righteousness, peace, and joy.

The promise of this verse is profound: "Whoever follows me will never walk in darkness, but will have the light of life." When we choose to follow Jesus, His light becomes our guide. It doesn't mean we won't face challenges or moments of uncertainty, but it does mean we will never be alone. His presence ensures that darkness cannot overcome us because His light is greater.

In a world filled with confusion and corruption, Jesus offers direction and hope. When we allow His light to shine in us and through us, we become a reflection of His truth and love.

The Lord is speaking to my heart to share, "Brace yourself for the exposure. God is showing you those who are not truly in your corner. Some are opportunists, and others are informants. Speak less and listen more. Those who have wrong motives will reveal their intentions as you let them do all the talking. Do not mourn the scorner, but rather rejoice that the devourer cannot eat up or stagnate your harvest."

The Attributes of Jesus

Day 6: Jesus, the Prince of Peace

"For to us a child is born, to us a son is given, and the government will be on his shoulders. And he will be called Wonderful Counselor, Mighty God, Everlasting Father, Prince of Peace."
– Isaiah 9:6

Peace can feel unattainable in a world filled with chaos, division, and uncertainty. Yet, in Isaiah 9:6, Jesus is prophetically called the Prince of Peace, a title that reminds us of His power to calm the storms of life and reconcile us to himself.

The peace that Jesus gives is not the temporary or superficial kind that the world offers. His peace is deep, lasting, and transformative. It surpasses all understanding, guarding our hearts and minds even when circumstances remain difficult (Philippians 4:7). This peace comes from

Nichol Collins

knowing that through Jesus, we are forgiven, loved, and held securely in His hands.

When Jesus entered the world, He brought with Him the promise of peace—peace between humanity and God, peace within our souls, and the hope of eternal peace in His coming kingdom. As the one true God revealed in the flesh, He made a way for us to be reconciled to Himself by removing the barrier of sin through His sacrifice on the cross. In doing so, He brought us into oneness with Him, allowing us to live in harmony with our Creator.

As the Prince of Peace, Jesus also calms the internal chaos we experience in times of fear, doubt, or pain. When we turn to Him in prayer, He fills our hearts with His comforting presence. His peace doesn't always change our external circumstances immediately, but it changes us, giving us the strength to endure with faith and hope.

Whether you're facing external challenges or inner turmoil, look to Jesus, the Prince of Peace. Let His Word steady your soul and His Spirit calm your heart. Today your mental state and

The Attributes of Jesus

inner emotions will be stabilized in Jesus name ! Peace be unto you !

I am led to tell you today, "Place both hands over your ears. Declare, 'I close and seal the portals of chaos.' The Lord says, take in worship music today and keep the lines of communication over the telephone at a minimum. There is something the Lord wants to speak, but being too chatty can drown out the small inner voice."

Nichol Collins

Day 7: Jesus, the Way

"Jesus answered, 'I am the way and the truth and the life. No one comes to the Father except through me.'" – John 14:6

There are countless philosophies and paths claiming to lead to truth and fulfillment, however Jesus stands as the singular revelation of the one true God. His statement in John 14:6 is both profound and exclusive: there is no other route to the Father, no other source of eternal life, and no other foundation for true purpose. Jesus, as the one true God in flesh, is the only way to salvation and reconciliation with Himself. In Him dwells the fullness of the Godhead, and through Him, we are brought into unity with God, receiving eternal life and the purpose He has ordained for us.

Jesus doesn't just point us to the way—He is the Way. Through His life, death, and resurrection, He bridged the gap between a holy God and

The Attributes of Jesus

sinful humanity. Without Him, we remain lost, separated from God by our sin. But through faith in Jesus, we are reconciled to the Father and granted access to eternal life.

Beyond salvation, Jesus also shows us how to live. His teachings and example guide us on a path of righteousness, integrity, and love. Following Him means walking in humility, trusting in His promises, and surrendering our plans to His perfect will. When we embrace Jesus as the Way, we not only find direction for our lives but also experience the joy of knowing we are on the path that leads to life everlasting.

As you reflect on this truth, consider whether Jesus is truly the foundation of your journey. Are you trusting Him to guide your steps, or are you relying on your own strength and understanding? Let His Word and His Spirit lead you into deeper fellowship with Him as your Father.

The Spirit of the Lord presses me to say, "Come deeper in my presence and stop doing everything so calculated. I want to interrupt your routine and impart greater strategy to thrive. You must be a risk taker to operate in the realm of faith for expansion. I am the Way follow me and win."

The Attributes of Jesus

Day 8: Jesus, the Truth

"Then said Jesus to those Jews which believed on him, If ye continue in my word, then are ye my disciples indeed; and ye shall know the truth, and the truth shall make you free." —John 8:31-32

Truth is often distorted in a world where opinions and perceptions can overshadow reality. Jesus stands as the one true Truth—the ultimate and unchanging standard by which all things are measured. As the manifestation of the one true God in flesh, there is no falsehood, deception, or contradiction in Him. Jesus, as the embodiment of truth, reveals the nature of God and the reality of His kingdom.

Through His words, actions, and sacrifice, He shows us the depth of God's love, the seriousness of sin, and the assurance of salvation for those who believe in Him as the one true God. Unlike the shifting philosophies of the world, Jesus' truth is timeless and absolute, offering us a firm foundation in a culture of uncertainty. His Word is the ultimate authority for our lives, guiding us in righteousness and equipping us to discern between right and wrong.

When we align our hearts with His truth, we experience freedom—freedom from sin, confusion, and the lies of the enemy (John 8:32). To accept Jesus as the Truth means to trust Him fully, submitting to His teachings and allowing His Word to shape our thoughts and actions. It is through this surrender that we find clarity, purpose, and a deeper understanding of who God is and who He calls us to be. As you journey through life, let Jesus' truth be your anchor. In a world filled with uncertainty, His truth never wavers, for He is the one true God, and in Him, all truth is found.

I hear the Lord saying, "Shut off every lie from the enemy. You know what I have deposited in your spirit, and you must war over the prophetic word spoken over you. The vision must be cultivated through planning and preparation to launch. Make strides towards your goal, and I will

The Attributes of Jesus

breathe on it. I am the Lord, and I cannot lie. Pursue, overtake, and possess it."

Nichol Collins

Day 9: Jesus, the Life

"In him was life, and that life was the light of all mankind." – John 1:4

Jesus is the source and sustainer of all life. From the beginning, He has been the divine force that brings life into being. John 1:4 reminds us that in Jesus, we find the life that enlightens and transforms us, shining into the darkness of this world.

Spiritually, Jesus breathes life into our souls. Without Him, we are lost in sin and separated from communing with Him. Through His sacrifice on the cross, He offers us redemption and new life. This spiritual renewal awakens us to our purpose, enabling us to live in freedom and relationship with God.

The Attributes of Jesus

Physically, every moment of life is a gift from Jesus, the Creator of all things. Each breath we take and every heartbeat reflects His sustaining power. He not only gives life but also provides for us, caring for our needs and guiding us through every season.

Eternally, Jesus offers abundant life that goes beyond the temporary. His resurrection assures us of victory over death and the promise of eternal life with Him. This hope transforms how we live today, anchoring us in the assurance that life in Jesus is filled with purpose, peace, and joy that cannot be shaken.

In Jesus, life is not just existence—it is abundant, eternal, and filled with light that overcomes all darkness. Let Him be your source of life in every way.

The Lord has led me to say today, "Be comforted in a dark world or in uncertainty. He won't let you fail as long as you stay in prayer and seek wise counsel from godly influences. The answer will be made plain. The blessed life is your portion—receive it by faith."

Day 10: Jesus, the Lamb of God

"The next day John saw Jesus coming toward him and said, 'Look, the Lamb of God, who takes away the sin of the world!'" – John 1:29

When John the Baptist declared Jesus as the "Lamb of God," he was pointing to Jesus' ultimate purpose: to be the perfect sacrifice for the sin of the world. This title connects to the Old Testament practice of sacrificing lambs to atone for sin, particularly the Passover lamb whose blood spared the Israelites from judgment in Egypt (Exodus 12:13). Jesus came as the fulfillment of that imagery, offering Himself as the once-for-all sacrifice to take away sin and reconcile humanity to God.

Unlike the lambs of the Old Testament, which provided temporary atonement, Jesus' sacrifice was perfect and complete. His blood not only covers sin but cleanses us entirely, making us

The Attributes of Jesus

righteous before God. Through Him, we are freed from the penalty and power of sin, able to stand blameless before a holy God.

This truth is the foundation of the gospel. Jesus, the Lamb of God, willingly laid down His life, taking upon Himself the punishment we deserved. His death and resurrection offer us the gift of eternal life, accessible to all who believe in Him.

As we reflect on Jesus as the Lamb of God, we are reminded of the depth of God's love and the cost of our salvation. It is not through our works or efforts but through the precious blood of Jesus that we are made new.

I feel an unction to release this word, "Be not deceived by man in this hour. Keep your focus on Christ and do not idolize those who appear to draw big crowds. The word of God is not mentioned on many platforms. Stay in the word and lay before Him as a sacrifice. Let nothing separate you from the Lamb of God. Discern His voice and tune out the strange fire."

Day 11: Jesus, the Vine

"I am the vine; you are the branches. If you remain in me and I in you, you will bear much fruit; apart from me you can do nothing."
– John 15:5

Just as branches depend on the vine for sustenance, strength, and the ability to produce fruit, believers rely on Jesus as the source of our spiritual life and growth. By nurturing our relationship with Him, we can live a life that reflects His attributes. Remaining in Jesus means abiding in His Word, walking in obedience, and staying in close fellowship with Him through prayer and worship. It's a daily relationship that nourishes our soul and equips us to reflect His character.

Without this connection, we become like a branch that withers—unable to fulfill our purpose . When we stay connected to the true Vine, our

The Attributes of Jesus

lives impact others for the kingdom of God. The fruit of the Spirit includes qualities like love, joy, peace, and patience (Galatians 5:22-23). Fruitfulness is not achieved through our own efforts but through the power of Christ working in and through us.

Jesus reminds us that apart from Him, we can do nothing. It is only by the leading of the Holy Spirit we can be effective, and tap into spiritual abundance. Let your life flow from the Vine, and you will see His power and purpose manifest in every area.

The parable of the vine and the branches makes it unmistakably clear in verse 6 that Christ did not support the notion of 'once in the vine, always in the vine.' Jesus lovingly warned His disciples that it is indeed possible for true believers to turn their backs on Him, fail to abide, and ultimately face being cast into the everlasting fire of hell. Hell, originally intended for the devil and fallen angels, has tragically enlarged itself due to the increasing perversity of the world.

I hear the Holy Spirit saying, "We have been given free will, and with it comes the responsibility to make sober decisions, resisting the allurements of the adversary. Our decision to refrain from sin stems from a deep love for God, not fear of punishment. Stay the course and abide in Him!"

The Attributes of Jesus

Day 12: Jesus, the Word

"In the beginning was the Word, and the Word was with God, and the Word was God."
– John 1:1

Jesus is the Word made flesh, the living and visible expression of the one true God. He reveals God's divine nature in human form. From the beginning, the Word was with God and was God, and through Him, all creation came into being.

In Jesus, we see the fullness of God revealed. His teachings, actions, and sacrificial death are not separate from God's nature but are the perfect embodiment of His will. Jesus' words are more than profound teachings; they are life-giving truth—the message of salvation that calls all to believe and be reconciled to the Father. His actions, from healing the sick to forgiving sins, display God's love, justice, and mercy, inviting humanity into relationship with Him.

Through Jesus, the invisible God becomes visible. He is the bridge between heaven and earth, showing us what it means to live according to God's divine purpose. Jesus is the way, demonstrating the love and power of the Father in every aspect of His life.

As the Word made flesh, Jesus invites us to experience the fullness of God's nature and His will for humanity. He is the ultimate revelation of divine truth, and through Him, we are brought into a transformative relationship. In Christ, we find not only the meaning of life but the very essence of the one true God manifest in the flesh.

I hear this in my spirit, "Let nothing separate you from the love of God. His word is your lifeline to differentiate the false and true teachings of Christ. If it's just a few verses a day, study them in depth to learn and not just read for formality. In a prophetic-driven church culture the Lord is also speaking through 66 books. Open the word!"

The Attributes of Jesus

Day 13: Jesus, Emmanuel

"The virgin will conceive and give birth to a son, and they will call him Emmanuel, which means 'God with us.'" – Matthew 1:23

Through the immaculate conception, God was birthed into the Earth to walk alongside His creation in a unique and profound way. The name Emmanuel, meaning "God with us," is a comforting title for Jesus prophesied in Isaiah 7:14, which was 700 years before the Birth of Christ. It shows that He came to live among us, not as a distant God but as a close and personal Savior.

Jesus' presence assures us that He is always near, no matter the circumstances. Whether we are experiencing joy or facing trials, His guidance, comfort, and strength are upholding us. In every season of life, He understands our struggles and shares in our victories.

Nichol Collins

This truth also proves that we are never forsaken. Emmanuel assures us that He is not unreachable and understands our daily fight of crucifying our flesh. Through the Holy Spirit, the presence of God continues to dwell within believers, making the promise of God with us an ongoing reality.

As we reflect on Jesus as Emmanuel, we can have solace in knowing that He resides within believers since the Day of Pentecost. Jesus brings His peace, love, and wisdom to guide us on the journey, expresses the essence of God's closeness with us, His continuous presence through the Holy Spirit, and the comfort we find in His constant companionship.

The Lord says, "Trust in His promises, He will always be with you, so look unto Him from where your help comes. Fear is not of Him, so elevate your faith in this hour."

The Attributes of Jesus

Day 14: Jesus, the Redeemer

"Christ hath redeemed us from the curse of the law, being made a curse for us: for it is written, Cursed is every one that hangeth on a tree."
– Galatians 3:13

To redeem means to buy back or to rescue from bondage. Redemption came from the practices of ancient warfare. After a battle, the winners would often capture some of the defeated. Among the defeated, the poorer ones would usually be sold as slaves, but the wealthy and important men, the men who mattered in their own country, were held to ransom. When the people in their homeland had raised the required price, they would pay it to the winners, and the captives would be set free. The process was called redemption, and the price was called the ransom.

Nichol Collins

Galatians 3:13 reveals the depth of this redemption: Jesus stood in our place and took the curse we deserved. Just as a ransom was paid to secure the freedom of prisoners, Jesus paid the ultimate ransom with His blood, setting us free from the captivity of sin guilt, condemnation, and death.

The curse is broken, and we are made whole because of His immeasurable love and grace. As we reflect on Jesus as our Redeemer, we are reminded that His blood was the price and His love the motivation. This incredible act of redemption calls us to live in gratitude and embrace the new life He has given us—a life marked by freedom, purpose, and an intimate relationship with God.

The Lord told me to tell ya, "Be of good cheer. You aren't under a curse, the test you've been facing is coming to an expiration. No demon in hell can stop your next season. The King has one more move to make!"

The Attributes of Jesus

Day 15: Jesus, the King of Kings

"On his robe and on his thigh he has this name written: KING OF KINGS AND LORD OF LORDS." – Revelation 19:16

Jesus reigns supreme over all dominion, both on earth and in heaven as King of Kings. Revelation 19:16 paints a vivid picture of Christ's sovereign rule at His second coming, declaring His ultimate power over all rulers, governments, and forces. There is no strength greater than His, and His reign is everlasting, unlike the temporary leaders of this world.

Jesus is the King who rules with righteousness and justice marked by perfect holiness, fairness, and truth. Unlike earthly rulers who can be corrupted by sin and greed, Jesus doesn't reign as an oppressor but with grace. His kingship is not only a future promise but one that is also present in the lives of believers today.

Nichol Collins

As we reflect on Jesus as the King of Kings, we are reminded that His reign is not just a distant promise but a present truth. His kingdom is one of peace, justice, and everlasting rule. We can take comfort in knowing that no matter the chaos of the world, Jesus is on the throne, sovereign over all things.

The Lord says, "I stand on the counsel of my own will. Haven't I done it times past? Stay in the realm of miracles and pray in the Holy Ghost. I want you to prosper, but can you stand to be blessed?"

The Attributes of Jesus

Day 16: Jesus, the Servant

"For even the Son of Man did not come to be served, but to serve, and to give his life as a ransom for many." – Mark 10:45

In Mark 10:45, Jesus redefines what true greatness looks like. Rather than seeking positions of honor or power, He came to serve. Jesus, the Son of God, could have commanded the adoration and service of everyone around Him, but instead, He humbled Himself to meet the needs of others. His life was a model of humility, compassion, and selflessness—values that run counter to the world's view of leadership.

Throughout His ministry, Jesus served in practical ways: healing the sick, feeding the hungry, and washing His disciples' feet. His example teaches us that true greatness is not found in being served but in serving others. Jesus calls us to follow His example, showing love, kindness, and humility in our interactions with those around us.

As we reflect on Jesus as the Servant, we are challenged to consider how we can serve others in our daily lives. Whether in our families, workplaces, or communities, we are called to imitate His selfless love and humble service, making His kingdom visible through our actions. Real ministry is done for the benefit of those ministered to, not for the benefit of the minister. Many people are in the ministry for what they can receive (either materially or emotionally) from their people instead of for what they can give.

I am led to encourage you with these words: "God sees the acts of kindness you have done. Sometimes, the ones you've blessed may not show appreciation, but the Lord has the receipts. The blessing is coming, and because you did it from your heart, a double portion is coming to your household in Jesus' name!"

The Attributes of Jesus

Day 17: Jesus, the Miracle Worker

"When Jesus landed and saw a large crowd, he had compassion on them and healed their sick."
— Matthew 14:14

This verse shows a powerful image of Jesus as the Miracle Worker. He did not turn away from those in need but, moved by deep compassion, He healed the sick and performed miracles that revealed God's power and love. Jesus' miracles were not mere demonstrations of supernatural power—they were acts of mercy that met people where they were, addressing their physical, emotional, and spiritual needs.

Jesus performed miracles to show that God's kingdom had come near. Whether He was calming storms, feeding thousands, or healing the blind and lame, each miracle was a sign of God's dominion breaking into the world, restoring what was broken and bringing hope to the hopeless. These miraculous acts were a reflection of God's heart to bring wholeness and salvation to humanity.

Even today, Jesus is still the Miracle Worker. While His earthly ministry may have ended, His power remains. Jesus continues to heal, restore, and transform lives through the Holy Spirit, working miracles in the lives of believers and demonstrating God's love and compassion. Whether in physical healing, emotional restoration, or spiritual transformation, the miracles of Jesus point to His ongoing work in the world.

His compassion for us remains, and He still works miracles today, showing us that nothing is impossible for Him. I hear the Lord say, "I will move for you according to the measure of your faith. Do you believe me for what looks difficult? I still can do what looks impossible. Use my name to resurrect dead dreams, a negative health report, or marital turmoil. I will do it for my namesake."

The Attributes of Jesus

Day 18: Jesus, the Advocate

"My dear children, I write this to you so that you will not sin. But if anybody does sin, we have an advocate with the Father—Jesus Christ, the Righteous One." – 1 John 2:1

An advocate is someone who speaks on behalf of another, someone who pleads their case. In this passage, Jesus serves as our intercessor, standing between us and God, defending us even when we fail. As our Advocate, Jesus is fully aware of our weaknesses and failures. He knows the struggles we face, and yet, He pleads our case with the Father, not based on our own righteousness but on His.

This advocacy is not a one-time act but an ongoing role that Jesus plays in the life of every believer. He continues to intercede for us, ensuring that we are not condemned but forgiven, as He represents us before the throne of grace.

Nichol Collins

His righteousness covers our sins, and through His sacrifice, we are declared innocent.

As we reflect on Jesus as the Advocate, we are reminded that no matter our shortcomings, we are never without defense. Jesus stands before the Father on our behalf, offering His righteousness as our justification, ensuring that we have access to God's grace and mercy at all times.

The Lord wants me to assure you, "I know your secrets and I love you in spite of them. When you turn from those things that hinder your progression, I am drawing you closer. The harvest is still being released because your heart posture is integral. Be at peace in this season, for the accuser, Satan, seeks to affect your health by carrying shame. Lay your failures at My feet, I love you," says the Lord of Hosts.

The Attributes of Jesus

Day 19: Jesus, the Friend

"I no longer call you servants, because a servant does not know his master's business. Instead, I have called you friends, for everything that I learned from my Father I have made known to you." – John 15:15

In John 15:15, Jesus offers us a profound invitation into friendship. He tells His disciples, and by extension, all believers, that He no longer calls them servants but friends. This is a revolutionary statement, for in the culture of Jesus' time, servants were not privy to their master's personal thoughts or intentions. But Jesus, in His love and grace, opens His heart to us, sharing with us the deepest truths about His kingdom.

Jesus, the Friend, does not relate to us from a position of distance or hierarchy, He invites us into a relationship of mutual trust and intimacy, where He reveals the will of the Father to us and we respond with love and obedience. He listens to our hearts, comforts us in our sorrow, and rewards our diligence.

His friendship is characterized by unconditional love, and He demonstrates the depth of that love through His actions. To be called a friend by Jesus is a humbling and empowering reality. It means that we have a constant companion, one who loves us without measure, guides us with wisdom, and walks with us every step of the way.

This analogy dropped in my spirit: just as a friendship among peers is expected to display loyalty, we should strive to exhibit a dedication to the Lord. It is much easier to please the Lord, who is one person, as opposed to church members, friends, etc. It can be draining trying to be a people-pleaser. Aim to walk in the Spirit, avoid fulfilling the lusts of the flesh, and remain steadfast in your kingdom assignment.

Day 20: Jesus, the Alpha and Omega

"I am the Alpha and the Omega, the First and the Last, the Beginning and the End."
– Revelation 22:13

Jesus declares Himself to be the Alpha and the Omega—the First and the Last, the Beginning and the End. These titles emphasize His eternal nature and sovereign authority over all things. The Greek alphabet begins with the letter Alpha and ends with the letter Omega, symbolizing that Jesus is the source and the culmination of all creation. Everything finds its origin in Him, and everything will ultimately be brought to completion through Him.

As the Alpha, Jesus was present at the creation of the world, and as the Omega, He will be there at the fulfillment of God's plan for the world. He is not only involved in the beginning and the end of history but is also actively present in every moment in between. Jesus is the eternal One, who transcends time and space, holding all of history in His hands.

This truth provides us with immense hope and assurance. We serve a Savior who is not bound by time or limited by circumstance. He is present in every season of our lives, from the beginning of our journey with Him to its eternal end. Jesus, the Alpha and Omega, knows the full picture and has the power to guide us through every moment.

I want to remind you, "He is both the author and the finisher of our faith, and His sovereignty over time assures us that nothing in our lives is outside of His control. Do not doubt, rejoice as if the promise has come to pass. Put your faith in action."

The Attributes of Jesus

Day 21: Jesus, the Judge

"Now there is in store for me the crown of righteousness, which the Lord, the righteous Judge, will award to me on that day—and not only to me, but also to all who have longed for his appearing." – 2 Timothy 4:8

The Apostle Paul speaks of Jesus as the righteous Judge, a description that carries profound significance. As the Judge of all humanity, Jesus has the authority to judge both the living and the dead, and His judgments are always just, fair, and rooted in truth and love. Unlike earthly judges, whose decisions can be influenced by bias or incomplete knowledge, His judgment is not random but is the result of His perfect understanding of our lives and motives. He calls us to live righteously, to walk in truth, and to reflect His character in our actions.

Nichol Collins

While Christ offers grace and mercy, He also calls us to live in obedience to His Word, knowing that His judgment will be according to how we have responded to His offer of salvation. Jesus, as the Judge, will hold every person accountable for their actions, thoughts, and the condition of their hearts. He expects his children to reflect His kingdom, with integrity, holiness, and love.

God says, "Your choices have eternal consequences so live with the awareness that you will give an account to the righteous Judge, who is also our Savior, Advocate, and Lord."

The Attributes of Jesus

Day 22: Jesus, the Teacher

"When Jesus had finished saying these things, the crowds were amazed at his teaching, because he taught as one who had authority, and not as their teachers of the law."
– Matthew 7:28-29

In Matthew 7:28-29, we see that Jesus' teachings stood apart from those of the religious leaders of His time. The crowds were amazed by His captivating authority, unlike the scribes and Pharisees who merely quoted others. Jesus spoke with divine confidence and wisdom, unveiling Kingdom revelations that had long been hidden from humanity. His words were not just rules or commandments; they were life-giving, transformative revelations that penetrated the heart and mind.

Nichol Collins

His wisdom was not just intellectual knowledge but a practical, impactful guide for how to live in alignment with His providential plan. Jesus' teachings still shape our lives today. They lead us in the path of truth, righteousness, and peace. When we seek to follow His teachings, we are not just gathering information; we are being transformed into His image.

As we reflect on Jesus as the Teacher, we are reminded that His words are still relevant and powerful today. They are the foundation of a purposeful life, guiding us toward deeper knowledge of Him. We discover love, obedience, and grace in a voluntary fashion.

I feel the Lord leading me to share this: "Do not assume you know everything. Rely on the Divine Teacher to guide you and provide counsel, even in decisions that seem simple. Remember, the Devil is in the details. Some of the biggest disasters arise from the smallest nuances. Have an ear to hear the Teacher, Jesus."

The Attributes of Jesus

Day 23: Jesus, the Lion of Judah

"Then one of the elders said to me, 'Do not weep! See, the Lion of the tribe of Judah, the Root of David, has triumphed. He is able to open the scroll and its seven seals.'" – Revelation 5:5

The Lion of the tribe of Judah is a symbol found in both Genesis and Revelation. In Genesis, Jacob blesses his son Judah, calling him and his future tribe a lion's cub and a lion (Genesis 49:9). In Revelation, the Lion of the tribe of Judah is declared victorious and worthy to open the scroll and its seven seals. Both Matthew and Luke affirm Jesus as a descendant of Judah, pinpointing His deity and His role as the true King to whom the long-awaited obedience of the nations belongs.

The Lion symbolizes not only Jesus' royal lineage but also His strength, courage, and victory. Jesus, the conqueror, triumphed over sin, death, and the grave, securing eternal victory for those who trust in Him. Through His sacrificial death and resurrection, He defeated the powers of darkness. No enemy, circumstance, or power can conquer Him.

As the Lion of Judah, Jesus embodies the power and majesty of a victorious King who fights for His people. His triumph ensures our victory, giving us confidence and hope, knowing that we share in His eternal kingdom. Reflecting on Him as the Lion of Judah reminds us that we are part of a victorious kingdom and that our King has already overcome all things on our behalf.

I sense in my spirit that you are about to triumph boldly over your fears. Like a lion, a symbol of strength, you are receiving a powerful push to step into your purpose. Though navigating the path to bring your vision to life has presented challenges, clarity is beginning to unfold, guiding you forward.

The Attributes of Jesus

Day 24: Jesus, the Intercessor

"Therefore he is able to save completely those who come to God through him, because he always lives to intercede for them."
– Hebrews 7:25

This verse, along with others like it, reminds us that while Christ's work to secure the salvation of His chosen ones was completed on the cross, as evidenced by His declaration, "It is finished!" (John 19:30), His love for us never fails and He remains our great Defender. This is the intercessory role He currently fulfills for those who belong to Him (1 John 2:1).

While Jesus intercedes for us, Satan, whose name means "accuser," tries to bring accusation against us, revisiting our sins and vulnerable areas before God, just like he tested Job (Job 1:6-12). However, these claims hold no credence in heaven because Jesus' sacrifice on the cross paid for our sin in full. When Jesus died, His righteousness was credited to us, and our sin was credited to Him. This is the great exchange Paul speaks of in 2 Corinthians 5:21. This act allows God to accept us as blameless in His sight. It is crucial to understand that Jesus is the one and only mediator between God and mankind. He did not ascend to heaven after His earthly ministry on "vacation" from His eternal role as the Shepherd of His people.

As our Intercessor, Jesus understands our struggles, weaknesses, and temptations. He is intimately acquainted with our human experience, having lived among us and been tempted in every way, yet without sin. Jesus provides us with the spiritual support and encouragement we need to keep moving forward in faith. I feel led to say, "You are covered!! No demon in hell can interrupt the divine orchestration of the Lord. Even the trials worked for your good and produce character. May your faith not waiver."

The Attributes of Jesus

Day 25: Jesus, the Rock

"They drank from the spiritual rock that accompanied them, and that rock was Christ."
– 1 Corinthians 10:4

In 1 Corinthians 10:4, Paul references the Israelites' journey through the wilderness, where they were provided with water from a rock. That rock, Paul reveals, was Christ. Jesus is not only the source of living water but also the firm cornerstone upon which we are called to build our lives. Just as the rock provided sustenance and stability for the Israelites in the desert, Jesus, as the Rock, provides stability, strength, and spiritual nourishment for us today.

Jesus is the unshakable pillar, no matter the challenges we face. In a world filled with uncertainty and change, Jesus remains constant, reliable, and immovable. He is the Rock that will never fail us, even when the storms of life rage around us. When we anchor ourselves in Him, we have a secure footing that will not be shaken by the trials, difficulties, or hardships we encounter.

Building our lives on Jesus as the Rock means trusting in His Word, and following His example. While He offers refuge. Reflecting on Jesus as the Rock reminds us to evaluate the foundation of our lives. Are we building on the shifting sands of earthly things, or are we grounding ourselves in the unchanging, eternal Rock that is Christ? In Him, we find a foundation that can withstand anything life throws our way.

I hear this song in my spirit,

"My hope is built on nothing less
Than Jesus' blood and righteousness
I dare not trust the sweetest frame
But wholly lean on Jesus' name

On Christ the solid rock I stand
All other ground is sinking sand
All other ground is sinking sand."

The Attributes of Jesus

Day 26: Jesus, the Bridegroom

"Let us rejoice and be glad and give him glory! For the wedding of the Lamb has come, and his bride has made herself ready." – Revelation 19:7

This relationship between Jesus and the Church is one of deep, intimate love and commitment. In Revelation 19:7, the image of Jesus as the Bridegroom is beautifully depicted. He is the Lamb who is preparing for the wedding feast with His bride, the Church. Just as a groom prepares for the union with his bride, Jesus is preparing His Church, His beloved, for His return.

Jesus, as the Bridegroom, loves the Church with an everlasting, sacrificial love. His love for us is pure, unconditional, and faithful. He gave Himself up for us, laying down His life so that we might be made holy and blameless before Him. His compassion is not passing but eternal, and it is this love that compels us to live in devotion to Him.

The bride is adorned with good works, love, and faithfulness, reflecting the character of the one she loves. It reminds me of someone under a evaluation in the workforce exhibits their best behavior for consideration of a promotion. Jesus' role as the Bridegroom is also a reminder of the ultimate union we will experience with Him. His return will be a glorious celebration, and we, His Church, will be united with Him face to face in eternal joy. Until that day, we are called to remain faithful, living with an eager anticipation of His return.

The Lord dropped in my spirit the parable in Matthew 25:1–13. Ten virgins take their lamps to meet the bridegroom. Five of the virgins are wise and bring oil for their lamps. The other five virgins are **foolish** and do not bring oil. The bridegroom is delayed, and the virgins fall asleep. At midnight, the virgins wake up and hear the bridegroom is **coming.** The foolish virgins ask the wise virgins for oil, but the wise virgins refuse. The foolish virgins go to buy oil, but **miss the bridegroom.** The wise virgins are rewarded, but the foolish virgins are

The Attributes of Jesus

disowned. The parable is a metaphor for the **preparation** of believers for the coming of Christ. The wise virgins represent those who lived **virtuous lives** and are **prepared for heaven.** The foolish virgins represent those who are unprepared and are **not allowed** into heaven.

Day 27: Jesus, the High Priest

"Therefore, since we have a great high priest who has ascended into heaven, Jesus the Son of God, let us hold firmly to the faith we profess. For we do not have a high priest who is unable to empathize with our weaknesses, but we have one who has been tempted in every way, just as we are—yet he did not sin." – Hebrews 4:14-15

The office of the high priest was established at Mount Sinai when God gave the Law to the Israelites through Moses. Aaron and his descendants were appointed as priests, tasked with interceding on behalf of Israel before God (Exodus 28–29). Among them, one was chosen as the high priest, granted the unique responsibility of entering the Holy of Holies on the Day of Atonement to offer a sacrifice that would temporarily cover the sins of the people.

The Attributes of Jesus

In Hebrews 4:14-15, we see Jesus revealed as our High Priest, bridging the gap between God and the human race. Jesus is the perfect High Priest because He is both the sacrifice and the One to whom the sacrifice is offered. As God Himself robed in flesh, He did not send another but became the atonement for our sins, offering His own life once and for all. Through Him, we have direct access to the fullness of God.

Jesus, though fully God, became man to suffer death and serve as our High Priest (Hebrews 2:9). Unlike earthly priests, He is called our "Great High Priest" (Hebrews 4:14), giving us confidence to approach the throne of grace for mercy and help (Hebrews 4:16). His perfect sacrifice and ongoing intercession assure us of forgiveness, healing, and closeness with God.

I hear, "Blessings are bestowed upon the righteous by the High Priest. Your sacrifice of labor, compassion, and servitude is not in vain. Look unto Jesus, the author and finisher of our faith. It is on its way—just rest in what has been promised in Heaven's courtroom."

Day 28: Jesus, the Fullness of God

"For in him dwelleth all the fulness of the Godhead bodily." – Colossians 2:9

Colossians 2:9 reveals a profound truth about the nature of Jesus Christ speaking to the divinity of Jesus, affirming that He is not merely a representative of God or an angelic being, but the very embodiment of God Himself. In Jesus, the fullness of God—Father, Son, and Holy Spirit—is made manifest. The Father in creation, the Son in redemption, and the Holy Spirit which dwells in us.

This truth is the core values of our faith. Jesus is the perfect revelation of God to humanity. Everything we need to know about God's nature, character, and will is revealed in the person of Jesus. In Him, we see God's love, holiness, justice, and mercy, all displayed in the most tangible and personal way possible. He is the

The Attributes of Jesus

visible image of the invisible God (Colossians 1:15), showing us the heart of the Father through His actions, words, and sacrifice.

When we look to Jesus, we are looking at God Himself. He is the fullness of all that God is and all that God desires to communicate to us. As believers, we are called to recognize the centrality of Christ in our lives, for He is not just a part of God, but the very expression of God in human form. Through Him, we gain access to the fullness of God's presence, His power, and His promises.

Reflecting on this truth reminds us of the depth of who Jesus is—God in the flesh. It calls us to worship Him, trust in His perfect revelation of God, and live in the fullness of His grace and truth. In Christ, we find everything we need: salvation, wisdom, peace, and life eternal.

Just as we are made up of body, soul, and spirit yet remain one person, our Lord, who is Spirit (John 4:24), took on a body to shed His innocent blood for the remission of our sins. He completed His earthly ministry with the promise of sending back the **Comforter** to empower us to reflect His attributes. While other religions worship multiple gods (lowercase "g"), we serve the one true and living Savior. Some things go beyond human understanding, but Revelation 4:2 declares that **ONE** sat on the throne.

May I submit to you that Satan isn't three persons, and neither is God!

Day 29: Jesus, One with the Father

"I and the Father are one." – John 10:30

Jesus boldly declares the oneness of God in both essence and function. The apostles were not preaching about three divine beings and were imprisoned, beaten, and FORBIDDEN to speak or teach the name of JESUS (Acts 4:18-20). He is not a separate entity or a subordinate figure; rather, He is the one true God, manifest in flesh. The Father, the Son, and the Holy Spirit are not distinct persons within a "trinity" of separate beings, but rather the one God revealed in different manifestations.

When Jesus says, "I and the Father are one," He is declaring that He is the fullness of God revealed to humanity. As believers, we understand that Jesus is the Triune God. Jesus is not one-third of God, but He is fully God—God incarnate—manifesting the divine will and nature in human form.

This truth has profound implications for our relationship with God. When we encounter Jesus, we are engaging with the one true God—manifested in the flesh to redeem us. He is the Father revealed, the Son who came to save, and the Spirit who empowers us.

The Oneness of God means that our salvation is rooted in the understanding that Jesus is the singular, all-powerful God who took on flesh to reconcile us to Himself. Through His death, burial, and resurrection, Jesus provided the way for us to be filled with His Spirit and brought into fellowship with the one true God.

Reflecting on this truth encourages us to look to Jesus, not as a mere representative of God, but as God Himself. He is our Savior, our Redeemer, and our very God. In Him, we find everything we need for life, peace, and eternal salvation, for He and the Father are one.

The Lord says to tell you, "Come into unity with Me and do not distance yourself because of

The Attributes of Jesus

insecurities or areas that need deliverance. It is I who heal, liberate, and sustain. Your success and contentment come through Me."

Nichol Collins

Day 30: Jesus, My Deliverer

I want to close with my testimony of who Jesus is to me and how I have allowed His attributes to be infused into my spiritual DNA. I was introduced to the LGBT community right out of high school, while suffering from rejection stemming from an offense that took place in church. The trauma of betrayal and isolation among my childhood church family devastated me, and the Devil used this situation to lure me into the clutches of sin.

I quickly began transitioning my appearance to portray a man. I cut my hair, grew sideburns, bound my breasts (which were never large anyway), and started wearing men's underwear and jewelry. I was young and clueless about how enticing this lifestyle would become. I dropped out of college and started partying all the time in West Hollywood, California, at gay bars and clubs. I drank alcohol and abused powder cocaine regularly. I almost died twice—once from

The Attributes of Jesus

alcohol poisoning and another time from an overdose on ecstasy. I was affiliated with a gang and placed in dangerous situations on numerous occasions.

The Lord, in His mercy, allowed me to escape with my life and a sound mind. It took time to be renewed in my mind. Walking through the progressive scale of deliverance required commitment to prayer, fasting, and changing my associations. I was the life of the party, but I had to come out from among those spirits I desired to be liberated from. I had to be off with people to be on with God.

I am not perfect, but I am not playing either. As of December 2014, I have not drunk alcohol, have been celibate for ten years, drug-free, and am truly content in my walk with Christ. The masculine behaviors from my transgender male persona have been eradicated. There is no residue of that lifestyle—glory to God.

I have authored over ten books, established a publishing company, Covenant Gear Apparel, and host a podcast. My website is globeshakers.com.

Nichol Collins

I am grateful for a fresh start and want this to be a sign to you that deliverance is possible! Keep a consistent prayer life, read the Word for yourself, and find a Spirit-filled church community to stay plugged in. God's continued blessings.

The Attributes of Jesus

Nichol Collins

The Attributes of Jesus

www.ingramcontent.com/pod-product-compliance
Lightning Source LLC
Chambersburg PA
CBHW070059100426
42743CB00012B/2600